Whose Vehicle Is This?

Whose Is It?

**A Look at Vehicles
Workers Drive—
Fast, Loud, and Bright**

by Sharon Katz Cooper
illustrated by Amy Bailey Muehlenhardt

PICTURE WINDOW BOOKS
Minneapolis, Minnesota

Special thanks to our advisers for their expertise:

Rick Levine, Publisher
Made To Measure and Uniform Market News Magazine
Highland Park, Illinois

Susan Kesselring, M.A., Literacy Educator
Rosemount–Apple Valley–Eagan (Minnesota) School District

Editor: Christianne Jones
Designer: Joe Anderson
Page Production: Amy Bailey Muehlenhardt
Editorial Director: Carol Jones
Creative Director: Keith Griffin
The illustrations in this book were created digitally.

Picture Window Books
5115 Excelsior Boulevard
Suite 232
Minneapolis, MN 55416
877-845-8392
www.picturewindowbooks.com

Printed in the United States of America.

Library of Congress Cataloging-in-Publication Data
Cooper, Sharon Katz.
Whose vehicle is this? : a look at vehicles workers drive—fast, loud, and bright / by Sharon Katz Cooper ;
illustrated by Amy Bailey Muehlenhardt.
p. cm. — (Whose is it?)
Includes bibliographical references and index.
ISBN 1-4048-1603-8 (hardcover)
1. Motor vehicles—Juvenile literature. 2. Motor vehicle drivers—Juvenile literature. 3. Air pilots—Juvenile literature.
4. Astronauts—Juvenile literature. I. Muehlenhardt, Amy Bailey, 1974- ill. II. Title. III. Series.

TL147.C64 2006
629.04'6—dc22   200502185

Start your engine and guess whose vehicle is whose.

Have you ever flown in an airplane high in the sky? Have you been on a boat splashing through water?

People use vehicles to get from one place to another. There are many kinds of vehicles. Some are slow, and some are fast. Some are loud, and some are quiet.

Many people use special vehicles to help them do their jobs. Can you guess whose vehicle is whose?

Look in the back for more information about vehicles.

4

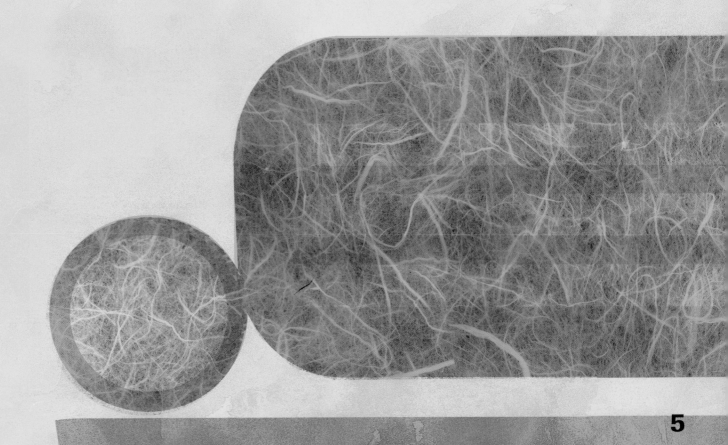

Whose vehicle is this,
carrying lots of children?

This is a school bus driver's vehicle.

The bus stops to pick up or drop off children.
A bus driver must be very careful to make sure
the passengers get on and off the bus safely.

Fun Fact: School buses are a yellow-orange
color. The official name of this color is
"national school bus glossy yellow."

Whose vehicle is this,
chugging down a track?

This is an engineer's locomotive.

An engineer drives a locomotive.
The locomotive pushes or pulls
the train down the tracks.

Fun Fact: The first trains chugged slower
than walking speed in the early 1800s.
Now trains can zoom up to 185 miles
(296 kilometers) per hour.

Whose vehicle is this, rushing toward flames and smoke?

This is a firefighter's engine.

A firefighter needs to reach a fire quickly so no one will get hurt. Fire engines have flashing lights and loud sirens. Those lights help everyone see the fire engine quickly and move out of the way.

Fun Fact: Fire engines carry ladders to reach up to high floors in buildings. They carry hoses for water. They also carry first-aid equipment.

Whose vehicle is this, flying fast
through the clouds and sky?

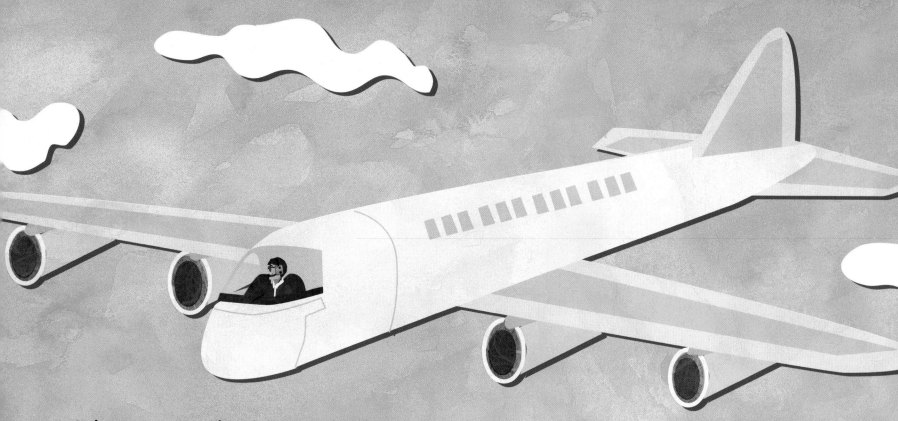

This is a pilot's airplane.

Airplanes travel very fast. A pilot must know his airplane well. He has to push many buttons, turn dials, and use the computer system when flying the plane.

Fun Fact: Some airplanes can carry as many as 700 people at one time.

Whose vehicle is this, making circles in wavy water?

This is a fisherman's boat.

A fisherman catches fish and sells them to markets. Those markets sell them to you. Fishermen need boats that are sturdy and strong. Their boats carry long nets and buckets for fish.

Fun Fact: Many fishermen's boats have refrigeration systems to keep the fish they catch fresh. This allows the fishermen to stay out at sea for several weeks at a time.

Whose vehicle is this, making lots of stops and drops?

This is a mail carrier's truck.

A mail carrier arrives at the post office early in the morning. Her truck is loaded and ready to go. She drives her truck from street to street. She delivers mail to every home.

Fun Fact: Most vehicles in the United States have the steering wheel on the left. Mail trucks have the steering wheel on the right.

Whose vehicle is this, blasting between stars?

17

This is an astronaut's spaceship.

An astronaut explores space. Before she goes, she exercises and takes classes to prepare for flying. A spaceship is built with special parts so it can fly into space and return to Earth safely.

Fun Fact: The moon is about 250,000 miles (400,000 km) from Earth. Even though a spaceship travels very fast, it still takes about three days to reach the moon.

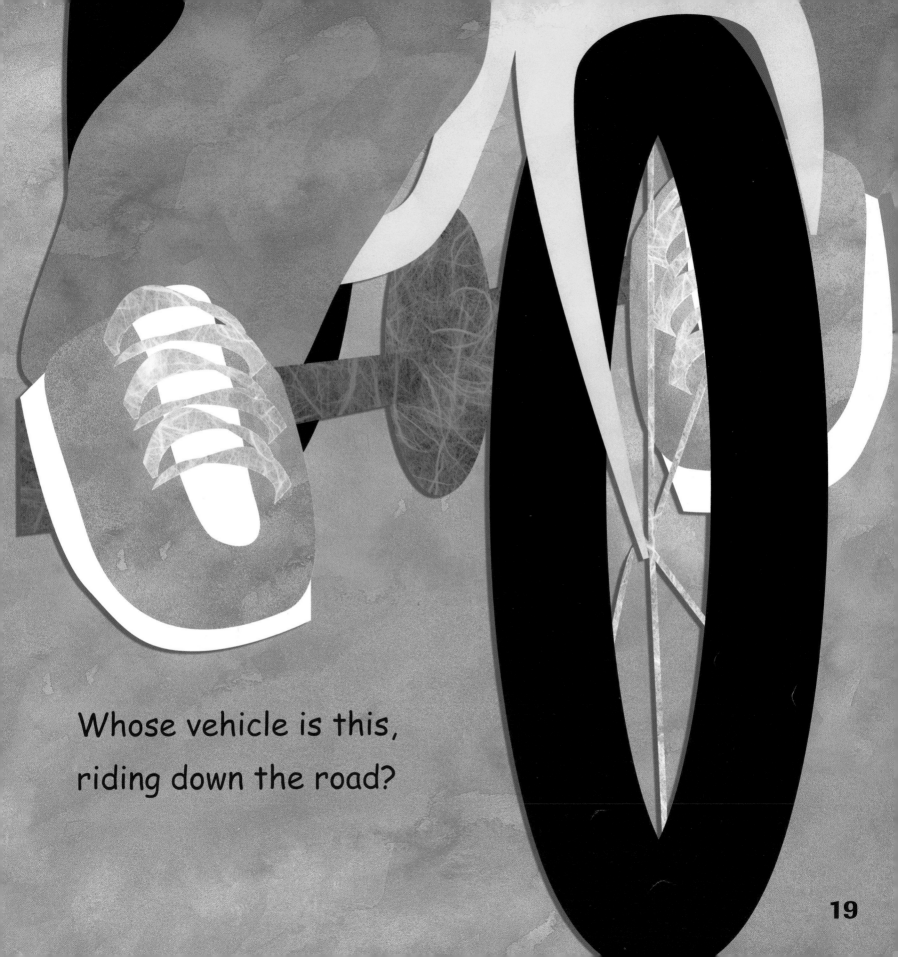

Whose vehicle is this,
riding down the road?

19

This is your vehicle!

It's your bicycle. People have been riding bicycles since the 1800s. In many countries, there are more bicycles than cars. How often do you ride your bike?

Fun fact: Bicycles are a popular form of transportation. Bikes outnumber cars two to one in the world.

Just for Fun

Whose vehicle is whose? Point to the picture
of the vehicle described in each sentence.

* I fly high above the clouds.

pilot's airplane

* I carry mail to each person's home.

mail carrier's truck

* I chug along on tracks.

engineer's locomotive

21

All About Vehicles

Cold Vehicles

In cold parts of the world, some people use dogsleds to travel. They attach a group of dogs to a large sled. The dogs can pull the sled over snow and ice.

Construction Vehicles

Construction workers drive different kinds of vehicles for different kinds of jobs. They use bulldozers for moving large piles of dirt. They use dump trucks for hauling dirt. They use pavers for smoothing streets. Every construction vehicle has a special job to do.

More About Mail

Over the years, the U.S. Postal Service has used mules, horses, dogsleds, trains, trucks, and camels to carry mail.

Up and Down

A helicopter is a special kind of aircraft. It can fly in ways airplanes cannot. It can hang in the air in one place. It can also move straight up and down.

Glossary

dogsled—a sled pulled by dogs

engineer—a person who drives a locomotive

locomotive—an engine that pulls train cars

outnumber—to be greater in number than something else

passengers—people who travel in vehicles

refrigeration—to keep cool

siren—a device that makes a loud sound

To Learn More

At the Library

Canizares, Susan. *Where Does It Park?*
    New York: Scholastic, 1999.

Royston, Angela. *Mighty Machines: Stories of
    Machines at Work*. New York: Kingfisher, 2000.

Schlepp, Tammy J. *Things on Wheels*. Brookfield,
    Conn.: Copper Beech Books, 2000.

On the Web

FactHound offers a safe, fun way to find Internet
sites related to this book. All of the sites on
FactHound have been researched by our staff.

1. Visit *www.facthound.com*
2. Type in this special code for
   age-appropriate sites:
   1404816038
3. Click on the FETCH IT button.

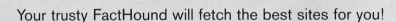

Your trusty FactHound will fetch the best sites for you!

Index

Look for all of the books in the Whose Is It? series:

Whose Coat Is This?
1-4048-1598-8

Whose Ears Are These?
1-4048-0004-2

Whose Eyes Are These?
1-4048-0005-0

Whose Feet Are These?
1-4048-0006-9

Whose Food Is This?
1-4048-0607-5

Whose Gloves Are These?
1-4048-1599-6

Whose Hat Is This?
1-4048-1600-3

Whose House Is This?
1-4048-0608-3

Whose Legs Are These?
1-4048-0007-7

Whose Mouth Is This?
1-4048-0008-5

Whose Nose Is This?
1-4048-0009-3

Whose Shadow Is This?
1-4048-0609-1

Whose Shoes Are These?
1-4048-1601-1

Whose Skin Is This?
1-4048-0010-7

Whose Sound Is This?
1-4048-0610-5

Whose Spots Are These?
1-4048-0611-3

Whose Tail Is This?
1-4048-0011-5

Whose Tools Are These?
1-4048-1602-X

Whose Vehicle Is This?
1-4048-1603-8

Whose Work Is This?
1-4048-0612-1